LITTLE OBLIVION

LITTLE

OBLIVION

SUSAN

ALLSPAW

ELIXIR
PRESS

DENVER,
COLORADO

PUBLISHED BY ELIXIR PRESS

PO Box 27029
Denver, Colorado 80227
www.elixirpress.com

Copyright © 2013 by Susan Allspaw
All rights reserved

Library of Congress Cataloging-in-Publication Data

Allspaw, Susan J.
Little oblivion / Susan J. Allspaw.
p. cm.
Poems.
ISBN 1-932418-47-4
I. Title.
PS3601.L465L58 2013
811'.6--dc23
2012036353

Designed by Alban Fischer
Cover photograph by Doug Bell

10 9 8 7 6 5 4 3 2 1
FIRST EDITION

CONTENTS

Introduction *vii*
Swallowing Antarctica *1*

I

Heading into Dion Island, Antarctica *5*
Naming the Bird *6*
A Song for the Peninsula *7*
Survival School *8*
Southern Ocean, Fairies, and Winter Solstice *10*
When Ice Catches Light, Addiction *12*
Not for the Krill *13*
The Body of Ice Remembered *14*
Comparing the Deserts *15*
Erebus Glacier Tongue *16*
Reverse Homesickness *17*
Going through the Gerlache *18*
McMurdo Spring *19*
Riverbed Warnings of Birth by Accident *20*
A Consequence of Irony *21*

II

What the Ice Knows *27*
Spring Run-Off and Underwater Time-Lapse Film *28*
Giving Up to the Southern Ocean *29*
Towing the Polar Haven *30*
Letter to the Mate on Watch *32*
Let the Ice Out *34*
The Beacon Valley *36*
Baring at the Bay of Sails *37*

Michelle at Hut Point *39*

Seven Attempts at Observation Hill *40*

Going to Pole *44*

Weightlessness in a Red Parka *45*

Turtle Rock, Antarctica *46*

Other Bodies *47*

Searching the Bow *49*

Burial *50*

A Consequence of Burden *52*

What Happens During Whiteouts in Antarctica *56*

Station Close, McMurdo Station *57*

III

The Rabbit Hole in the Ross Sea *61*

When Weather Moves In *63*

Dry Valleys, Erosion *64*

A Pebble in the Stream on a Sunny Day *65*

Going to the Seal Rodeo *67*

White's Escape Attempt *68*

Ross Island *70*

A Consequence of Solitude *72*

Observation Hill *75*

Searching for Fairies, McMurdo Station *77*

The Sound of Snow at the Pole *78*

Little Oblivion *80*

Lessons from Ghosts *82*

Saying Goodbye to the Continent *84*

Crack It Open *85*

Acknowledgments *87*

INTRODUCTION

In his essay "The Triggering Town," Richard Hugo makes a case for writing that does not rely on what's familiar and known; instead, he encourages poetry inspired by "triggering towns"—words, places, things free of personal associations that ignite one's need to write. If one stays within the realm of the familiar, Hugo maintains, "the imagination cannot free itself to seek the unknowns." The triggering town, being new and strange, sparks a curiosity that leads to emotional ownership:

> Though you've never seen it before, it must be a town you've lived in all your life. You must take emotional possession of the town and so the town must be one that, for personal reasons I can't understand, you feel is your town.

For Susan Allspaw, Antarctica is the ultimate triggering town. *Little Oblivion* draws on Allspaw's many trips to Antarctica, including her time working for the United States Antarctic Program aboard the research icebreaker *Nathaniel B. Palmer* and at McMurdo, South Pole, and Palmer stations. These luminous poems burst with vibrant images and sweep panoramically across mesmerizing landscapes while meditating on the human condition through deep and reverent encounters with the natural world.

As Charles Wright has said, "Narrative does not dictate the image; the image dictates the narrative," and indeed Allspaw's exquisitely textured poems are full of surprising images that capture the essence of Antarctica's stark beauty. In the world of *Little Oblivion*, we find nesting places for petrels, skuas, Adélies, and terns; an underwater home to baby krill, ctenophores, and salps; a terrain striated with sastrugi and punctuated by nunataks; a place saturated with such whiteness that "the sky bleeds into the earth / so that a whole body becomes a palindrome."

This connection to the landscape is at the heart of *Little Oblivion*. In the opening poem, "Swallowing Antarctica," the speaker is aboard an icebreaker and invites the reader to enter, as she does, fully and without reserve, to let Antarctica in and become part of it as it becomes part of you:

> if I were to jump...
>
> ...I would swallow all Antarctic
> relics, men and science alike, embody
> ancient ice and waters teeming with
> life, caught in evolution and frozen,
> a blueprint, a map on which to chart a course.

An eagerness emerges to both engage with Antarctica's history and to create a symbiotic relationship with the environment. This relationship resonates throughout the book, as something essential is often transferred between the natural world and its inhabitants. In "Not for the Krill," a diver named Jenny dives because "if she could, / she would breathe water." While submerged, "her breath becomes part of it all, / an even exchange." Reciprocity leads to true communion with the natural world:

> This is not about the krill or their numbers.
> This is about what a moon sounds like under ice,
> what a coyote howl will do to a current moving east.

Little Oblivion is also a place of dualities, opposites, and contradictions. Here we find excess and restraint, absorption and reflection, absence and presence. Even the title contains dichotomy. Pairing the word "little" with "oblivion" creates a sense of intimacy and boundary, while at the same time conjures an affection, as though "oblivion" were a term of endearment. Antarctica becomes a liminal space, residing in between extremes, like the ice shelf seen in "Ross Island":

> It is the shade of gray we never think about,
> the place we always stand between yes and no,
> solid but malleable, risky.

Another duality captured beautifully in the book is that of internal and external landscapes. The extreme weather in Antarctica literally forces people inside, but also to hunker down and look inside themselves, to connect with their innermost emotions. In his essay "Landscape and Narrative," Barry Lopez describes the interior landscape as "a kind of projection within a person of a part of the exterior landscape."

This projection and intertwining of internal and external landscapes are central to *Little Oblivion*: all the reflective surfaces of snow, ice, and sea act as mirrors, and all the open space, isolation, and long days lead to reflection on one's life. After climbing and reaching the top of a lookout point near McMurdo Station, the speaker surveys the land below and sees "the mirror of the plateau that shows everyone's true face." And in the poem "Observation Hill," when the speaker thinks about leaving, she recognizes the deep introspection Antarctica induces:

> With thousands of miles
>
> between us, I can easily pretend the ice shelf
> isn't still reflecting my indiscretions back
> as easily as a magic mirror.

As much as Antarctica functions as a giant mirror to reflect and illuminate the self, true to its dichotomous nature, it can also be a place to get lost and hide, as "hiding becomes easy in a town with / giant hoods, big pockets, and wool blankets," as well as somewhere to take sanctuary from back-home troubles, "the white keeping everything else / outside." Here, there are plenty of places to bury one's innermost secrets. Antarctica can absorb it all, become a vault in which one can lay to rest what haunts most, as in the poem "Burial":

> ...we are not so different,
> the ice and I. We hide secrets under miles of ice, covering a
> multitude of sins, and the land,
>
> guilty or not, knows when the glacier streams
> meet the ocean they will float a moment on that new ecstasy

> and then crack open

In addition to the cathartic release, the "cracking open," there is also a sense of transformation, even redemption here—"that new ecstasy." Something about Antarctica—the astounding landscape, its haunting beauty, its remoteness—draws people who are looking for something, "some last-ditch chances / at redemption… / some way to return to what we left / as whole."

As Jacques Cousteau has said, "From birth, man carries the weight of gravity on his shoulders. He is bolted to earth. But man has only to sink beneath the surface and he is free." The sea is to Cousteau as Antarctica is to Allspaw—in *Little Oblivion*, many who come burdened to Antarctica, including the speaker, leave feeling freer, lighter. Here, on Earth's southernmost continent, amid glaciers and ice shelves, the speaker finds clarity and an ability to soar, to rise above earthly concerns, as in the poem "Weightlessness in a Red Parka," where despite heavy layers of clothing, she feels weightless:

> This is what I mean when I say
> I felt weightless in all those clothes—
> that the water, wind, sunlight, all lifted like wings
> of skuas, terns or petrels, carried me through.
> When I say I was a red bird down there,
> I mean I had the way to see it all.

Leaving Antarctica induces a "reverse homesickness," a "snowbound ache." The speaker wonders how long it will take to "get the ice out of [her] fingerprints." In the end, she realizes it will always be there, a longing that will endure, as in the final poem "Crack It Open," which brings the narrative full circle:

> We are with it, in all its
> fallen glory, the ice. Our bodies
> cracked and weeping for open water.

If Richard Hugo is right, and "triggering subjects are those that ignite your need for words," then *Little Oblivion*'s Antarctica is a shining example of what a triggering town, in the hands of a skilled poet like Allspaw, can become. "When you are honest to your feelings," says Hugo, "that triggering town chooses you." Antarctica has most definitely chosen Allspaw to safekeep its stories. "White will follow me everywhere," says the speaker in one of the poems. After reading *Little Oblivion*, white will follow us, too.

Teresa Leo
Judge, Elixir Press Annual Poetry Awards

for Marc

SWALLOWING ANTARCTICA

When we round the bend in Charlotte's Bay,
when the bow breaks through ice like sugar
candy in a child's hand, when light breaks
over snow-capped mountains like a heaven
or a miracle, I prefer this side,
starboard, where the sun licks first, and where,
if I were to jump, I would not be missed for hours.
And if I were to jump, catch an ice floe
and ride it north, or sink into that sky
where penguins fly, I would swallow all Antarctic
relics, men and science alike, embody
ancient ice and waters teeming with
life, caught in evolution and frozen,
a blueprint, a map on which to chart a course.

I

HEADING INTO DION ISLAND, ANTARCTICA

Twenty centimeters of ice below the bow,
seven knots, and the barometer falls on us like bad news.

Writing the dead is not easy when we are on the way
to count penguins and their eggs, fathers

standing proud with their loads on their feet, snug and kept.
Emperors will fight to be fathers, even if they have to steal

an egg from another. Pity we all aren't like that. Pity dead fathers
can't see us trawling for science, wanting to write home

and say, Dad, the sun rises in the north here, and the Southern Cross
is pointing with us, south, where we will census

what hasn't been born yet. I can't reach him through the salt water.
Sea smoke, my father. Brash churned with tide.

NAMING THE BIRD

What do you call the giant petrel
flying just out of reach of the bow?
I call it the doll I lost when I was seven
between funerals.
I call it Billy Higgins, high school crush
lost to shyness and years.
I call it lost virginity, lost rivers,
lost bones of the dead.
I call that petrel by name: bird,
omen, father.
I call that bird every weighted phone call.
I call that bird an eyelash wish.
I call it a parole hearing,
an easy labor and birth,
an easy shot.
I call that bird a survivor.
I call it lighted darkness,
my named nightmares,
the ones I cannot lose.
I call it seen, observed, logged,
made public.
I call it holy, sacred,
unreachable.
I call it freed slave.
I call that bird my mother's lost breasts.

I call that bird my aching loneliness,
surrounded by thousands of mists.

SONG FOR THE PENINSULA

What gray silent shouts at horizon, what
harpy penguins swimming in the wake,
what final day-long dusk along the Drake,
a master of ceremonies at a loss for words.
Curved spine of land is gripped like a lover
to the Southern Ocean by ice, depths of
teen-aged tongues lapping the shore.
Blue calves into blue; tabulars lose
their virginity, and if I could walk out
among the bergs, float in the giant
ocean air on pack ice, I would be
the current lapping on hull, the song
of weather just off horizon; I would be
the darkness just beyond the bow.

SURVIVAL SCHOOL

Today, the herbie will blow but not bad enough
to warrant retreat, and digging trenches in the ice shelf—
a glorious education in physics. The blocks
weigh, and lifted in place,
they love gravity through miles of ice.

The tent will hunker toward ice
as close as it can, cocoon us, make us emerge
in the morning changed by a night full of frost-lit dreams.

Tim will take a walk along the flagged route.
He will talk with strangers about his wife and their problems—
to Silver City and back,
to shelter and back. He will
bring it all to bed with him, into the tent,
hoping to hatch free of it.

This is a place of transformation.

If we could see through
the blowing snow, just off the route we would see
other shelters where people have emerged,
changed, heroes of a sort.

It is only the first month of the season. If I
were a non-believer, I would say nothing
could be shed this easily, with boiled snow-water
and fleece-lined bags.
Out here, it is easier to believe you can speak away your fears,

let them hang on the air in front of you, fall
to be buried by the next storm.

Not quite to morning, the wind stops blowing and sunlight
opens to the Sound, glittery and whispering.
We will all emerge having dreamt and lost

our deaths, having grown ice for bones, snow for breath.

SOUTHERN OCEAN, FAIRIES, AND WINTER SOLSTICE

Count your blessings to see the pancake ice
forming solid floes before the ship, clouds
with silver linings and fairies darting
between salty frost flowers. Only angels

see the ice growth overnight, only fairies
can find the fissures before they split open
and let the moon through. We find a place
beside a floe, dig a hole, dig two. Take samples.

The scientists are looking for magic
thermodynamics wrapped in frazil ice,
mixed layers in water columns, baby krill
grazing on the underside, a miracle current

to follow on a down line. The scientists
are taking optics of ice cores, fluorescence
of phytoplankton—they are looking for light
to appear as it did in the beginning, the way

we're told the beginning was. On the Solstice,
the air is filled with sea smoke, the sky
without twilight an eerie, alien place. What happens
underneath that blanket while we play
in the sauna, run to the bow thinly clad with our cameras,
thinking only of that light that sparks beyond
the moon, without a hint of sun, that place
we all return to, like childhood, like the first time

we rode a bike alone? If we could be under there without apparatus, how would we light it?

WHEN ICE CATCHES DAYLIGHT, ADDICTION

Edges like a salt lick. Snowflakes
big as father's hands. Ice sheets

in herds moving in front of the bow.
Like sheets hot with love, they keep us

buoyant, filled with riding current
that must be like that beginning of sex,

slow breathing, air colder than any part
of the body, and when the equilibrium comes,

equally air and water, we steady
into it. Step in—it will not pass,

frozen again, the swell on the horizon,
until our four hours are up,

twilight moves on, and we are left
naked ridges between floes, melted

solid and smooth, gathering
moonlight with all our strength.

NOT FOR THE KRILL

Jenny dives because if she could,
she would breathe water, light photosynthesizing
through ice, that inverted pillow.
She is looking for science, but when that seal
pokes his head through the hole, she knows
he is looking for her, that he is not looking to feed or mate.
He knows she is not looking for krill, or ctenophores,

but for the current-cushion just below the ice,
slow wave of breath like the beginning of birth
or moon walk. She stays down as long as she can,
watches ribbons frozen in that ceiling, laughs,
because when she does, her breath becomes part of it all,
an even exchange.

When she surfaces, she will have a net filled
with baby krill and salps, ready to observe, dissect,
count. This is not about the krill or their numbers.
This is about what a moon sounds like under ice,
what a coyote howl will do to a current moving east.

THE BODY OF ICE REMEMBERED

for C. M.

At Razorback, the diver whose suit has leaked
is having a bad day, but tomorrow looks
more promising for him: the dive tenders
are young and their faces tell him
they're excited about everything they see—smoking Erebus,
distant splashes of seals making new holes, even the slush
forming on top of the dive hole that they must keep skimming off.

Tomorrow he will go to the ice edge
and jump in with both feet
with a girl's face hiding just behind his concentration.
His body will sink in the water
because when he isn't in it, he is loving that girl
in Colorado, swimming through her,
all her parts.
                He only wants to touch her
this time, right now, 50 feet below the surface
but his hands are claws in a dry suit
and keep him from clutching anything.
Even water moves through them,
leaves no trace. His breath always
hangs on the underside of ice, the other lover,
the one he keeps returning to. If only that girl
in Colorado could grow like a glacier, if only
she could move with the freedom of icebergs.
If only he could stay down, below the surface,
his breath forming a body on its underside, then hands
wouldn't matter, then deep water would be enough.

COMPARING THE DESERTS

Sand is not just broken glass and pebble.
It is a frightened nightmare, storm of rapid aging.
It is sarcophagus and hiding place.

In the Antarctic desert, the snow is infallible,
forms walls of glass, impenetrable hearts.
Both sand and snow drive erosion, the wearing down

of parts. Our bodies are like that,
maps of carved riverbeds, dry for years,
hollow mountains and disguised crevasses.

Shells that were once people revel
in the storm, an easy excuse to cover up
and hide that they have been changed,

that they are air in parkas, open wounds,
sinkholes, reckless empty skies. They dance
their invisibility, because blizzard

is as close to monsoon as we can get,
an easy, air-filled drowning.
Loss is inevitable.

We miss when we are here—
Oh, thunder,
oh, terrible rainstorm.

EREBUS GLACIER TONGUE

By November, the caves have finished weeping,
and the sun has turned ice crystals into cancer,
strange shapes, a mother's ovary.
The dawn-glow inside the caves
wants to be water, wants to know how to swim.
There have been people here; boots
knocked over the water, shattered it.

In the evening, the scientists dress
their warm-blooded bodies, trample
over snow and rock,
turn their flashes on as they step inside
and remember their births, breathing underwater,
the moment before the giant push,
rush of air. They all want
to touch the walls, break off a piece
to keep, a souvenir.

This is not the point; they are not part
of the story. Only the dry sobs
as winter leaves, as the ice predicts
its birth, its self-loss.

REVERSE HOMESICKNESS

Atlas returns to the ice. It is cold, the sun is almost up,
and he jokes about holding the world on his shoulders,
doing a headstand at the Pole, getting frostbite

on the tip of his bald head. Another world map
stretches across the polar plateau for him; he has left
behind a woman who loves him, who wanted him

to leave. Here, where horizon challenges his idea
of a straight line, where hearts are lonely nunataks
dressed in white, allowing the world to weigh on him

is a rosy burden of consequence. This ice cap
suits him, clings like an anxious crow call
to a field of scarecrows. When he returns

to the world of green and harvest, busy streets
and the unlikely plan of frostbite, he will wonder
where all his numbness comes from. He will find

the woman has laid her burden down, moved
on to other dressed-up hearts, and he is left
with miles of frosted sorrow, snowbound ache.

GOING THROUGH THE GERLACHE

First bergs at noon. We will put the Zodiac into the water, divers
and all. Under water like space, like the inside of a saguaro during
monsoon, the divers will catch baby krill, video the blue sky

of ice above them, breathe bubbles into water that could have touched
everything in the world already, but hasn't.
The ice remakes itself, and while the divers find small comfort

below the ice, we walk on water—
immersion far away for us. We are left out, old and dry.
All those stories of men who die at sea

waver in the slight breeze as we pass through the Gerlache Strait;
they, consumed by water. The divers in their dry suits
drown in the air around them, and we swallow what is left

when they surface. We move south to Marguerite Bay
where we fill our lungs with ice, swallow
continents of burden, seas of endless ache.

MCMURDO SPRING

Potholes love like the rest of us—
they absorb runoff like alcoholics on a Friday night,
holy divots, brown birdbaths. For the skuas,
this spring is the time to love water, forage for treasures
in trash bins, rain chicken bones on the town for a week.
              On Sunday, the ambulance answered a call—
heart attack out by the pressure ridges. A man is down.
Spring day, perfect for skiing,
but he may have been looking at Mt. Discovery too lovingly,
or maybe he could feel the sea beneath his feet, small god moment
too large to take. Or maybe his heart felt the need to push up
and out like those ridges of ice, so much pressure on either side,
the release when they reach up like small plants,
a relief when the sun finally hits them.
              Or perhaps he had a weak heart,
and the skuas are just hungry, and springtime here
is the same as every other springtime, filled with mud
and birds, pressure that can push anyone to drop.

RIVERBED WARNINGS OF BIRTH BY ACCIDENT

The rocks are chain-linked to the sides
to prevent them from sliding during dust storms.

No water here, Salt River, dry and filled with summer
brush, haphazard monsoon shrubs that want

that coffin of current over them, to be plump
with permeable membranes, dancing slower

than the desert air ever allows. On the Southern Ocean,
the rocks are free to roll where they want,

crash at boats they believe are god-imposters,
yell when the gale will cover their sounds.

There are signs along the riverbed, warning runners
and risk-takers of flash floods, the dangers

of walking where water wants to be. In order
to read the signs, the heroes already have to be in it,

waiting for that momentary drowning, breathing quick
with the belief that when it comes, it will pass

right through them, create deities and dead men
and men cured with salt, reborn rough and bitter.

A CONSEQUENCE OF IRONY

1

The moment I notice the linoleum valley
with dirt from small feet, grain of sand
on the cheek that sparkles in light,
I am human and have eyes. And if not eyes,
then toes to grip with. If not toes,
then a soul, the thing that hides when I need it,
holds words when I can't, hides in between ice floes.
I want to catch a floe south,
ride it like a free taxi to my end, until walls of ice
softly bump the ride. This is where I will find warm
milk and a god who listens and acts,
and, if I am lucky, sleep.
I believe in the scarcity of hair, how it pulls out
with repeated conditioning in the shower,
long strands that cross grout and tile in Rorschach pictures
before snaking down the drain—river snakes, holy adders.

I take a shower to shave my legs
because maybe smooth legs will lullaby me to sleep.
I pull the razor once, think of sun rays and stingrays
on ocean currents. I watch my body
turn red with heat, watch
this body, pale feet and hairy toes, red
indentations where clothes pressed too tightly,
fingers that wrinkle with time. I watch
this body not sleeping and count
the non-slip strips in the bottom of the tub.
I let the holy baptism begin, and pray for the water

to turn to dreams, pray the rivers running over
breasts are holy rivers, Nile or Amazon, Niangua in
someone else's religion. Onyx, the southernmost river.
I pray a lot because I only have vocal chords
between sunrises. I want
to have a night long enough for purpose.

When I bear a cross that far, south,
I make a point of sorrow,
to ruminate upon it. This can't merely be
a wall of ice—it must be the barrier to heaven, or a harmonious
resting place for fools. I complete
one task to move on to another. There are others like me
who travel to find heavy lids, answers, medicine to make them well.
The burden of leading them is on my shoulders.
The angry procession will let down a rope long enough
to be a painter and ask me to climb it—and without crampons
I will ascend, white-dressed and lighthearted,
because thick rope is a task well done, no matter
where it leads. I climb.
Beyond the consequence of irony,
crossing circles with tangents and smiling zebras, and a chain of ghosts
who called their sleeplessness a sickness.
I did not embrace the beauty of continual day. One without,
a lack, I have turned into leader, and with my jaw clenched,
accept the position. The line behind grows longer,
and while there are no TVs, there is ice enough for tragedy.
I will not have to look under building rubble or
burning bush, but I will need a longer rope, a longer tether.

2

In the infinite moment of a life of a dust particle
landing on a strand of hair, the sea—
The sea and its creatures wave me in, begging down the steel hull

of ships and crooked mizenmasts. There is never a cause
for drowning beyond grief or sorrow, a horseback swayed with burden,
the sea. Its zebra stripes of current call and take, and take again.
Some have called it mighty,
but I call it mother, womb, home,
briny winter coat of frost flowers.

When I reach the volcano, relief.
I am sure this is the last task to God.
I think He is my goal. Past crevasses, over snow bridges.
I am lighter than human now, but that could be my eternal nightshirt,
blowing in the wind and smoke from the caldera. A veil
of smoke now—a macabre bride. I could be the fourth
traveler if only someone would ask for my truth. Near the top
I pass plane wreckage buried in snow. I expected this.
No confessions or penance, no buried sins, only empty pockets
of air below crusted surfaces, waiting for a strong enough gust
to blow them back to air. I cross myself
for rose petals and their smells up there, wish to see the happy face
of Erebus as a sacrifice is offered. But like all tasks,
sacrifices are just out of reach. My fingers rock a lava bomb like
a lullaby, like an orphan on his first night with new parents.

From the top of the volcano, I extend south
and ask for a ride through crevasses. There is no more rope.
Now, it is up to the angels to bring me where there is only one direction
to go. All that white like heaven must be a dream,
and if it is a dream, then I will be sleeping. I know
a good mirage when I see it, and even when frosty wings
drop me cleverly like a pin head beneath a compass, I know.
Beneath frozen eyelashes, here will be
an audience with God, because He has to be in a place like this.
This is the lone great expanse of white, lonely as a zebra's barren belly
where all stripes lead. If there is no God here, there will be no rest.

How long will it take to scrub this long climb out
when I return, to get the ice out of my fingerprints?
It sinks in like ink, clings. I imagine
scrubbing blubber-smoked faces, black soot
moving around in water, turning the pure to soiled, transference of sin.
It is always this way with water, but not without cost.
Three bathtubs full per man, I think, and wash my pale
clean skin, wash the clean off, hoping maybe dirt will put me to sleep.

II

WHAT THE ICE KNOWS

Ice clings,
wants the way around melting.
People fall in love with it,
great lovers gliding over
each other without friction,
without jagged edges
and hidden mammoth
foundations.

Even ice over ice creates heat,
melts rough faces
into smooth century-skins,
re-freezes into something
macabre, the terrifying
beauty. We get
lost in that imaginary horizon,
the space where we must
believe in infinity or die
trying to find it.
When we leave,
it clings, the damn child,
the obsessor, the stalker.
The ice never learned to let go.

SPRING RUN-OFF AND UNDERWATER TIME-LAPSE FILM

December brings melting sea ice and mirage,
fata morgana against low clouds.
Reasons for coming to this lost continent
disappear in the run-off of this old mountain town;
the routine is hard here, easy to fall out of step,
fall off a precipice like Vince. They stopped erecting crosses
years ago, left bodies on mountaintops
for monuments, let Antarctica absorb all the dead,
no fighting it. She'll win every time.

Easy to relate to the dead here
and search all day for chains around my ankles:
I receive an obituary over email. Babies are born
or miscarried somewhere else.
A friend's heart is breaking as his love leaves him
for solitude at the Pole—I care as much
as a birch would stand against this weather,
white, peeling, invisible. This white
will kill me if I blink too fast.
Instead, try to block it out
and remember what stars are like, the moon,
full-faced and brilliant, the moon. Beneath the ice,
a slow motion world moves and is swallowed. Static, it seems,
despite the mud flowing downhill in the now-spring,
static and unbreathing as starfish seem,
until the urchin has no escape.

GIVING UP TO THE SOUTHERN OCEAN

When everyone needs to throw their anger overboard
or let go of all the swallowed Antarctic beauty,
they go port side, sunset on homeward journeys.
Port will hide you when you need hiding,
when the ship has beaten you until you cry,
and good sailors don't cry, except by the port rail
on 02. The darker side of the ship, its
left hand, unnoticeable, secret. If there is any
desperate jumping, it will happen from this side,
a silent splash, a stoic leaving behind.
It holds all lost lovers and dead fathers,
all Antarctic winter nightmares, all sailors'
bad premonitions. If you wrap it in silent screams,
the ocean will accept it all, light the forward way.

TOWING THE POLAR HAVEN

The haven is more like a summer camper than anything,
blue canvas stretched on a frame for divers to keep warm.
Christian calls this work with a smile, invites a few of us
into the orange Sprite for a Sunday drive.

The tracks kick up snow like middle school boys
after a blizzard, first day back to school with all they have
to prove. The tracks make it easy
for anyone to follow us. The tracks leave witness, until

we make it to Armitage, see the blue haven waiting
for us to tie it up, begin the hour trek
to the unnamed iceberg that has caught
itself in seasonal ice just off Cape Royds,

on holiday for the summer. Almost
the whole town will make pilgrimage to it
at different times, as if it were a Mecca
or a Jerusalem, as if it could hold all our unwanted

secrets. Like grandmothers in graves, this iceberg.
Its split on the side provides us our thrill for the day,
no real danger, but when I walk in between those walls
of ice, run my hands over the smooth frozen surfaces,

I imagine being in a crevasse, my feet pointing toward
nothing, my eyes reaching for the blue sky, unable
to catch it and haul myself up. I walk through
because it is a passage, and this is what we do down here,

make all these rites of passage, day in and out, without
hot coals or wet dreams, although there are some of each.
On the other side, I can barely hear the men drilling into the ice
to secure the haven for tomorrow's dive, barely hear the photographer

walk around the berg, kneeling close to the sunbathing crabeater seal
for a full-face shot. He is making his own confessions
to the ice, and when I walk around the other side, when
Christian shows me how to pull the rope through a v-hole

with a drill, I have made a small peace with the berg,
paid my homage, offered my loyalty. I have made
my connection, with moist fingertips and glacial ice,
silence in the impossible beauty of crevasse walls.

When the haven is secure, we have no more excuses
to stay. We head home and I imagine all the tracks
around the berg, and hope, soon, they melt out;
soon, the ice reclaims its own.

LETTER TO THE MATE ON WATCH

Paul, the bridge is a quiet place tonight,
and you like to guide the ship with the lights off,
the glow of radar and GPS on your face,
reverse sunrise. This winter, the ice
hides all hints of ocean swell, but when the ship
is still enough, I can see your body sway; ocean
has worked its way into your bones.

I should have known you
back on Revere Beach Parkway,
the way I knew Friday nights in Tina's Olds,
cruising, not sure what we were looking for.
You would have been there,
all brackish and scented with sand,
spray, and that sweet odor
that only twenty-something guys can have
around teenaged girls. We wanted to be
those Lolitas, with our hair and jeans
just right, the speed past Kelly's Roast Beef
slow enough to turn heads if we wanted,
slow enough for those boy-men to catch us.
Everything rode on Friday nights.
Our lives depended on hearing the surf slap the sand,
and if we stretched hard enough, we
felt that pounding between our legs
when we rode past guys like you,
when we silently begged to be followed
and were, when we made the U-turn before Wonderland,
came back, rode by like the tide,

all tired and restless.
                         Out here, the ocean hides
everything Friday nights were about. You
are as far away from that tide as the desert, as
covered with ice as the path ahead of us.
Paul, out here there are no Oldsmobiles, no Lolitas
waiting for you. But there are miles
of ocean for your taking. Miles of swell beneath you.

LET THE ICE OUT

On top of South Pole dome, the risk
is no more than being found.
The edges of the silver earth cap
extend beyond the frame of the photo;
for people who don't know the Pole,
Peter may well be anywhere. He can fool
them into believing he was up there
or not. There were pretenses to climbing up—
cleaning antennae, checking satellite
connections.
                    But Peter, what is the truth
beneath each step that defies gravity
at its strongest? Why reach the top
only to climb down? Your body
is obstinate, wanting
the weightlessness you think you'll get
up there, you the cloud, the erect windbreaker,
conqueror of triangle dome steps,
nothing more.
                    When you return to the States
you will pass the picture around
like a baby, brag
about the danger, the risks,
but Peter, wasn't the risk coming down
back to that starting place full of weight,
and wasn't the continent your body
up there, defeated, restless?

Come down, Peter.

Let the ice out of your body.

THE BEACON VALLEY

Farthest west, the valley folds up
like the hand of a grandmother, offers shelter
to what geologists will call soil to simplify things.
Look, the geologist says, the frost polygons
on this side. Yes, he thinks he can hike over
to them from camp. Eight-million-year-old ice
under here, he tells us, oldest ice in the world.
After we've taken all the pictures
we can, we make our way back to the helicopter,
our arms loaded with ventifacts and other holy rocks,
and the geologist reaches down, touches the soil
like it is the head of a child crowning,
an eight-million-year-old baby. The day is warm,
and his breath does not hang in the air. It moves
into soil he smells to remind him
of a Missouri backyard childhood.
He will only stay five days, put
pieces into vials, love it and cringe
every time he takes a step. When the clock says night,
he will write to his wife, tell her how beautiful
this rock, the formations, tell her because if he does
he won't feel guilty about not wanting to leave,
guilty for loving it the way he does.

BARING AT THE BAY OF SAILS

Layers were easily shed on the beach.
We felt the warmth on bare feet,

forty degrees of sand, no wind,
only the sound of melting snow on cliffs

behind us. Naked, we couldn't take our eyes
off of the pressure ridges, off of each other.

Nothing as beautiful as two women hiding
from the world on the southernmost nude beach,

frozen sea and distant seals the only witnesses.
Sand between shoulder blades, feet dodged

snow patches. We needed this, even though
we giggled as we set the timer to take the image,

our nakedness as wonderful as icebergs.
We clung to boyfriend memories like baby blankets;

easy to forget how comforting another sorrow
can be, how easily it can be shed for an audience

of seals. When we heard the helicopter engine
and ran for our clothes, we felt lighter,

as if we left all that emptiness imprinted on the sand,
as if we left it for no one to find for years,

as if we left it because we knew the wind would cover it up.

MICHELLE AT HUT POINT

At the Point, Michelle wears her hood
because it's cold and no one can see her
face thinking north, to Ketchikan, Alaska,
its timber, mountains with trees, and Ben,
and Ben's hands. Michelle stands
as still as birch, oak if the wind wasn't blowing
like raven wings. Discovery Hut is buried in snowdrift
so its ghosts are silent. Michelle wonders
if her companions will miss her when she goes
to Ketchikan in her deep hood, fur fringe blowing,
hands pulled up into the sleeves. If she pulls far
enough, she can feel Ben's in there, too,
feel roots grow out of her feet, plant her
in a place that needs trees and can't have them.

SEVEN ATTEMPTS AT OBSERVATION HILL

1

My second day on ice. The rest decide
to hike to summit. We dress for cold air
and wind, like Antarctic birds, all feathers
and desire. We think it will lift us up,
this climb, a good omen for the season.
It falls like heavy boots in snow, like men
on the plateau searching for the Pole. They
had their obstacles, too, and when I reach
the half-way mark, turn my back on the rest
and watch town, with all its hidden faces,
I understand the need to turn back, save
what can be saved, walk back to what I know.
    I head down the slippery slope. I think
    today was not the finest day for climbing.

2

Today was not the finest day for climbing,
but I had to swallow something, and air
was as close to success as I could get.
Not Olympus, but nearly, as remote,
as god-holding. If this could be a win
I could survive the last three months of sun-
light and Pole-breath making hackles on my neck.
Sometimes it is enough to stare up
at Scott's cross and the cloud-catchers who climb
every day. Every day they find something
new on the sea ice, new skua egg, new
path around what they have run away from.

     Hiding becomes easy in a town with
     giant hoods, big pockets, and wool blankets.

3

Giant hoods, big pockets, and wool blankets
won't keep me warm on these days, wind blowing
hard to find summer. They say the weather
will improve next week; all signs point to melt.
That means the zig-zagged path I watch each dawn
(if I can call it that) will first be ice,
then mud, then dusty rock as bad as snow
that first day. I prefer the cold, when I
can use excuses the size of coffee
mugs, long underwear, secrets told under
the safety of pillows. This place was made
for poetry and death, photographs and
     immortality. I've climbed for four months.
     I have cried out, climbed until my lungs bled.

4

I've cried out and climbed until my lungs bled
the whispers of dream-telling, secrets out
on Sunday afternoons full of penance
and reconciliation. God was not
part of the plan for my South, but then I
should have known better. Everyone seems to
be looking for him in every crevasse,
every nook. Even the chapel. Where, then,
was he when I was in the dark at sea,
begging for some light? The ones with faith say
he was there, in the pack ice, waiting for
me to see him. But even the faithful
     here look north when they need a better day.
     We all walk up like sacrifices.

5

We all walk up like sacrifices,
and when we reach the top, above the fog
and all the breath of town, we call it even,
a draw, and beg the continent for
a few more days, some last-ditch chances
at redemption, or civility, or
some way to return to what we left
as whole. When I get up to where my breath
has evened out, where I can feel the weight
of Scott's cross and its implications lift
like someone else's soul, over the Sound
and out, the way an arctic tern's might,
    I take a thousand photographs in lieu
    of words. Love, I cannot even speak here.

6

Of words and love, I cannot even speak,
breathless at the sight of open water,
small layers of clothes, almost setting sun.
The end of season is near, and had I known
what I could have found on the top of Ob,
I would have made the effort sooner, found
strength to look farther out, to the mirror
of the plateau that shows everyone's true
face, the mountains that make valleys full of
life and mummies, the continent that hides
her best secrets. The chest is open now,
broken open like a flood, and it cries
    the best cry of recognition, dead
    speaking to those left, those finding their way.

7

Speaking to those left, those finding their way
down the hill, I find rocks more slick than words.
In seven days we will all be farther
north, surrounded by green. What will we say
when people ask us how cold it was?
If it was hard? If, somehow, we found what
we were looking for? I will crawl back down
into my parka, into the deep lung
climb it took to get me to the top, not
only blood and breath and ancient memory
but steadfast men with faith who went before.
When they ask me if I will go back, if
    it was hard, I will tell them, after
        my second day on ice, the rest decided.

GOING TO POLE

Inland, light dances
with wind, but nothing moves.
Ken says three days
is never enough,
time a strange shoe to wear
around that cup of earth.
He goes down,
plants his feet flat
on the edge of one hour,
then another,
wraps himself in tomorrow
and tries to run off his time.
It is all sweat and light,
all night sunlight.
The sun stays up,
a minute is still a minute,
and a man chasing his tail
around a pole
is only chasing a shadow that does not grow.

WEIGHTLESSNESS IN A RED PARKA

If feathers evolved to encourage flight,
why do so many keep us warm and gravity-tied
to these dirt roads, corrugated buildings
not meant to keep heat in, well-worn paths
that zig-zag to Ob Hill summit?
                                        I'm surprised
we are all as light as we are, despite the sun
reflecting off all our skin surfaces, despite
the weighty moods of winter-overs.
    But some magic must be woven
between patches and reflective swatches;
in all those pockets, there must be air to hold us up.
On the Armitage loop, I walked on water
for hours. I lay in a seal's old cradle, ready to curl up
for my own hibernation. On Ob Hill, I thought
if I lifted my arms, the wind would carry me like
a weather balloon, like an albatross, circumnavigating
the south, never reaching a new day.
                          This is what I mean when I say
I felt weightless in all those clothes—
that the water, wind, sunlight, all lifted like wings
of skuas, terns or petrels, carried me through.
When I say I was a red bird down there,
I mean I had the way to see it all.

TURTLE ROCK, ANTARCTICA

A short climb
but difficult, a black
back of island, shell-shaped,
a volcanic trick of time.
Easy to climb halfway up,
let numbers work
the way they work,
slide down half
the distance, then gain
half, and lose again.
The top seems inevitable.
The heroes climb;
they think it will bring them
closer to the world through light.
The wildlife know better.
Seals stay at the edge of the sea—
for them it is an edge.
A man who climbs
is still searching for borders.
Eventually, he will hoist himself up
like the seals at the broken ice edge,
win the battle with numbers.
He will think, infinity.
He will realize, nothing.

OTHER BODIES

At Pegasus Field, laying sideways
as an awkward old man in a hospital bed, a fuselage
attempts breathing. It has been in this position
for years. The helo pilots ignore it
as a bad omen when they fly to Black Island.
The Navy presumably left it, not worth
the salvage, better to let the ocean have it
when it's ready.

The continent chooses which bodies to bury,
like the crash on Erebus, like the two skiers who fell
too far into a crevasse to save. Aching moments, those
of the taking,
              like watching the *Endurance* sink time
and time again. Like hearing last words echo off ice walls.

On the side of Erebus, rescuers attempted to retrieve the dead,
wishing the plane crash back in time like a tape on rewind,
put the pieces of the DC-10 and bodies together and tell them
not Antarctica, not today. Today Erebus has tricks
up its sleeve, veils around its head too thick
for even the best pilot to see through. Today
they will all die, tragedy second only to the haunting memories

of rescuers who have to climb up, for the remote
chance of life, for evidence.

There is no morgue in McMurdo.
When someone dies here, his body is stored in the science freezer.

The scientists want to protest; their samples, their work
is next to a dead man. They don't complain.
The whole town will talk about it in hushed tones and code,
until the plane comes and takes the body home for an American burial.

And then there are the other bodies, shells of people
who walk not quite like zombies and not quite like angels
through the town, over snow ridges, across frozen
seas. They are living their own loss, not much different
from Americans in Boston or New York or Kansas,
except for the mirror of macabre beauty before them,
except that they can see their way back to whole—
a continent filled with crevasses must have some small offering of salvation.

SEARCHING THE BOW

What better place than forward, where the waves
fall first and all ship's pitch and roll originates?
What better place for birds to ride thermals,
hovering in the space a ship will occupy in seconds,
the low hum of engines better than a lullaby?
At night, the Southern Cross just off the port corner
makes everything clear: we are headed south, toward
the calming slices of ice, the noise of motion
as this ship carries its cargo through all different kinds
of seas. When you stand up here, the wind passes through
you as if you were a ghost. When you stand and gaze
at the night sky, nothing can touch you.
On the bow, you become the breaker of ice,
crack that open emptiness beneath you.

BURIAL

In a plane south, I drown out every noise
with noise, except the quiet of my blood vessels, eyelash blink,
and the questions I lift up with as much strain

as it takes to lift this LC-130 Hercules off
the ice: what kind of secret is enough
to ride to the South Pole

to bury, what ache drives a woman as far
as this? How, when the Sound calls me to like open water
and asks me to revel in its raw

nakedness, even beneath the sea ice,
I could even begin to answer it—the ice is trying
to tell me a secret it's been keeping

for years, the secret I whispered
in one of those moments alone, inside a parka, the secret
that scared me to even utter.

If the ice screams it back
I can hide it somewhere, or else allow some stranger
to bear witness to it, make it real rather

than a bottle only I know about
buried in a thickness of snow and ice measured only
by the ability of aircraft to land on it.

The secrets are, after all, from me. This

is a place to capture the bottle and bury it deep in a drill hole
in a glacier, wait ten thousand years

for it to float out into open water. Make, finally,
my mark on this continent, not with scars or other signs
on a body, but the way a lover

left easy leaves a mark, the way a happiness
leaves yearning, the way pleasure
lifts off like a plane without insulting gravity—

I give the ice my mark. I give it my mark and take
my own as a happy burden, as a bundle meant for me to carry
despite slowing the world.

This is what I was waiting for—
Earth's gravity to take me as strong as it can,
the best answer to a simple problem

of physics. And when we fly over the Trans-
Antarctic mountains, and the streams of glaciers roll away
from them as easy as the moments

after lovers have been fulfilled, we are not so different,
the ice and I. We hide secrets under miles of ice, covering a
multitude of sins, and the land,

guilty or not, knows when the glacier streams
meet the ocean they will float a moment on that new ecstasy
and then crack open, not unlike Pandora's

box. So too, the friction between glacier and land,
the love between them in a thin shimmer
of water, becomes catalyst, dust, and burial.

A CONSEQUENCE OF BURDEN

1

I do not sleep, so this story does not go much
farther than my bed, my Antarctica of down on top, fits of sweaty
sheets from the effort of closing my eyes. Every time they close
I am there—Erebus, Royds—and every time, the land is unreachable. Like
    the man
who fell too far in a crevasse to be saved but not far enough
to die quickly, I carry this burden like another wooden cross
erected for the sleeping dead. I can see Bishop's imaginary iceberg
floating without cause, and restlessness keeps it afloat.

I am Antarctica's burden to carry, one more lost child
looking to bury myself on the return trip, to resurrect a hero to save me
from myself. Down there, women aren't heroes—they are the ice,
silent and begging, silently stoic in the carrying of burdens. They
are the boxes all fears are buried in, boxes with six months of darkness for locks.

When sleep comes, it is with clenched jaws and migraines
jumping ropes of skull muscle. All of the ropes
have slipped in and out of my hands, and when I grasp,
as firm as unripe mango, I swing to find sure footing.
The strands of my hair braid themselves into strength.
Where did they come from? They answer—
because in my nights of wakefulness, hair speaks—we have come
from your drain. We have returned to attempt rescue.
Are you ready to be rescued?
                          I hang.
The imprints on my palms, all the lines that are supported to hold
fate and future lives, feel them tickle into movement.

I thought flesh would at least be a constant.
                              This is what I was looking for,
wasn't it? Atonement, safety, rescue, penance?
If I let go, who will catch me? If I let go,
am I ignoring my true rescue? If I stay, will I seal a life
of hot showers, sleeplessness and longing into my palms?

In the desert, the sand can trick the toes into believing they are floating.
And when it rains, there are glorious hallelujahs sung from every crack
of skin. In the rainforest, there is different singing—sunlight
the lonely wanderer everyone wants over for dinner.
Weather will not rescue me any more than hair could.

I am getting forgetful,
forgotten deodorant more than twice this week, and almost
forgotten my phone number and emergency brake. Forgetfulness is a sign
of fatigue, they say.
                       And if I want to paint my nails,
they will look as if a child has painted them, or an impressionist
who is near-sighted, red splotches that bleed into cuticles.
I go to bed but don't sleep. That is obvious.
The possibility of colored toes, of toe art, of art spreading
across my body, engulfing buttocks that already prevent me
from wearing those clothes I used to wear, when I was younger,
when I slept. I try not to be foolish when I reach
for the teddy I've had since ten, remember when it still
had a tag, when there wasn't a hole under its chin.
There was never a time it didn't have tears soaked into its hide.
I am not ashamed I have never washed it. I've turned
into a little girl again, compulsively braid my hair before going
to bed, light the rice paper covered nightlight, set the house alarm,
pray the ghosts will save me from the lunatic living.

If I were a coyote, I'd howl.

2

After another night has begun, I am tired of doing the chasing.
God seems to be taking a pass; this task is not beyond
my own strength and I know it.
Under the down, with hair that has been wet, braided, unbraided,
knotted and dried, I think about horses and crevasses,
cacti and Scott tents. Then, a change—fear
buried in depots for the return trip, because without fear, a journey
couldn't have joy, and joy is perishable.
Tonight I will count happy animals. Armadillo. Wombat.
Bat. Sea star. Hyena. Turtles without wide roads to cross. Surprisingly, rats.
This is only the short list. The ark will require more thought.
Thought keeps me up.

I have a plan: After the last zebra stripe runs itself off, I have a solid-
colored horse. My cynical side reminds me a zebra is still a zebra
without its stripes. It will never be horse. I want to save the zebra who,
in one version of dream, gets shot down by a spear again and again.
In another, the zebra saves me from drowning. I want to return
the favor. I want to be seen as a savior. Remember the false gods clause,
my day voice says. You'll never get to heaven that way.

Even as the days get longer, even though
the sun stays up longer, I blink with daydreams.
I thought the darkness
and the rain were keeping me up, as if they had a louder sound
than sunlight. But even now, after weeding the garden
and forgiving the spiders that make their way into the house,
I fidget when the clock says I should be rolling over,
putting an unconscious arm around my lover, falling
back into whatever dreams will take me. I
imagine noises in the attic, make stories of raccoons,
or crazy roof-walking men. I check the house alarm.
I will not shut the light off tonight.

Three loads of laundry, four bills, one phone call.
I count things on my to-do list like sheep. The reminder
of unfinished things pricks my right hip with sciatica.
Maybe the dead on my wall are begging to be written alive again.
I have already written them over and over again.
I count the women, the dead,
back until I start counting those who aren't dead yet,
but will be soon. When their faces reach my head,
I do not say their names out loud. I do not want
to jinx them or make it seem they are already lost.
Even though my eyes are closed, I cry.
I carry the images of beautiful faces as long as I can bear it.

WHAT HAPPENS DURING WHITEOUTS IN ANTARCTICA

Demitri, don't worry about the planes or their wings;
in this wind, they will stay on the ground, unmoving and gray
even behind the whiteout. In the meantime, brush the weather
from your sleeve, pinch off the frost
from your lashes. This place is your magic box, the one
you always wanted to open when you were a child
but never did, always afraid of disappointment.

When you cut the block of snow, make it small enough
to love, and when you surround it with all the other blocks,
make sure they all love it right, stacked close, stacked
to kiss the wind and turn it around. The camp
belongs to us, the white keeping everything else
outside—what matters is this gloved hand,
these tent stakes, WhisperLite stoves.
Soon we will crawl into tents, drink
hot drinks, eat. If the weather were kind,
it would stay this way for days.

Around the perimeter, green flags.
You can see four before they drop out to white shadow.
Yes, they lead to a road, and that road to people
and tasks, all the things
that keep us tired. But here, in this horizonless
corner, we are awake, breathing
and tingling with warmth from good work.
You could touch everyone here.
The tents are strong, but thin.
Everything in the night will come through,

frost to rain on our faces.
Make sure to touch it all, Demitri.
It could disappear as easily as we have.

STATION CLOSE, McMURDO STATION

It must be the sensation of Atlantis,
when the summer season
finds its way out, off the ice, before
the sunset lasts longer and longer,
nothing to stop it. When Atlantis sunk,
I imagine people fled, swam before dark
waters consumed them, too.
The galley must be a ghost town,
Gallagher's a hole for alcoholics,
the brave winter-overs and stragglers
waiting for the last Herc flight.
Every season is long with work,
hikes, boondoggles to places around Ross.
The moments for breathing are few and far between.
Most of the rooms are closed up, shades pulled,
shells of what once was raucous laughter,
stories of dives, dry valleys, tents
caught in windstorms. All of the chocolate
and coffee has been given to winter-overs
or stored for next year's crew. To walk through
is like walking a cemetery street, left-over
echoes caught in old belongings, things left behind,
things abandoned. The ice is like that;
like the toy from seventeen Christmases ago,
the broken and lost one, the one
that will never leave you.
By the time the last flight is called,
it is a miracle we all have not drowned,
caught up in the vacuum of sinking.

III

THE RABBIT HOLE IN THE ROSS SEA

This hole is smooth and tinted blue
down to the slush; beyond the mirror,
another universe, an easy escape.

Put your face at the edge
so you smell salt, remnants
of ice, new ice being born.

Look to the bottom,
40 feet, 50, where light
shouldn't reach but does
and shows you a sea star
you can touch, as distant
as stars, a distant Orion.

Easy to jump in,
breathe water warmer than air.
The escape is what matters,
getting to the other side
of the ice, knowing its bottom
as sky.

Today, no one will jump.

Even though falling in
is a possibility, even though
this land holds nothing we can take,
in this hole, wonderland stops.
When we wake up,

the snow in our boots melted,
we return to traffic and newspapers,
Antarctica will be our looking glass.
We will wish we had jumped in
when we had the chance.

WHEN WEATHER MOVES IN

Inside a day like today, in a place like
South Pole, when the sky bleeds into the earth
so that a whole body becomes a palindrome,
head reaching for sky or earth or sky,
an easy pause can turn a breath into frost
words to finally describe this: a blind invisible trip
to the peak of the earth's curves, desire
built to convince the smallest snowfall
that it is meant for beauty, fear made
to entice prayer from everyone, to any deity,
guilt designed to ensure the burial of all
the dark secrets that come here. Consequence
is as large as the polar ice cap, and the best I can do
is touch the earth the sky the earth and beg, and beg again.

DRY VALLEYS, EROSION

The glaciers still push hard, so old
they have names: Taylor, Ferrar, Erebus.
Land as old as this carries an imprint
of those walls of ice, an old woman
whose hips never forget the mark of birthing.
Age frays a heavy weave, wears things down.
At night the ice-rivers moan over land
like new lovers, eternal and never tired.
The valleys cradle them like children,
love them on their slow approach and retreat.
Here, the frictionless land is silent,
like a widower who still listens
for footsteps, the morning whistle of his wife
before breakfast, her breathing next to his.

A PEBBLE IN THE STREAM ON A SUNNY DAY

Something glass or ice is lying broken in the road,
reflecting someone's bad luck sunlight
coming from the north, morning sunlight,
the kind that lasts a four-month long day.
No luck in McMurdo, Antarctica, only circumstance
where a piece of glass or ice can sit
in a dirt road all morning, getting beaten
and broken with traffic.
                        On this day, work is postponed
and we all emerge from buildings with spring in mind,
armed with plastic bags and gloves
to pick the daisies: cigarette butts,
plastic bags, and soggy cardboard boxes
that have made their way into ditches, rusty nails
that hide by edges of stairs—all of our leftovers
shaken loose when another day-long hour is beginning
and a woman's feet just won't work on the staircase
anymore. At her computer, she forgets
about the mountain peaks across the Sound
or the clear blue water opening up in Winter Quarters Bay,
and pulls at her eyelashes, hoping maybe for blindness
or bald eyes, or that any of those wishes lying on her desk
will come true.
                        In the stream next to Building 175,
the woman finds a rock, half green, half black, volcano rock,
more luck to add to the pile she has accumulated
on her desk, in her room, artifacts
that only need belief in order to transform.
When the rock is underwater, it sparkles as though it is dreaming

of spider webs and tree shade. If her hands stay in the water
long enough, the woman can imagine she hears
leaf rustle. If her hands stay in the water long enough
there will be another ache demanding her attention.
Down there, under Antarctic summer run-off,
everything has potential sparkle, everything has the potential
to be remnants of a volcano.

GOING TO THE SEAL RODEO

There are two holes cut in the ice: one for the seal,
one for the people to watch him.
It's not enough to find him, let's call him Bob,
because all good broncos have names,
not enough to simply watch from the observation tube.
Even seals have things they want to do in private.
The scientists are ready to catch Bob
and saddle him with a camera
so they can watch all his sub-ice wanderings,
what he eats, which females look good to him,
how he runs in fear from orcas.
Bob surfaces at the hole, hoists himself out
into their hands. The rodeo has begun.

Before they are finished, Bob will lie still with sad eyes
saying he has been abducted by aliens. Without mirrors,
he will forget that he has expensive equipment on his back,
run into walls, bump the bottom of the sea ice, eat
with his mouth full. The scientists will write it all down,
make it a typical week for Bob. And when he finally comes back
and they remove the camera and he swims back into the water,
he feels lighter, like a woman who has just cut inches off of her hair,
like someone who has confessed, like someone who has quit his job
and gone looking for seals in Antarctica
and found himself strapped to the back of a seal.

WHITE'S ESCAPE ATTEMPT

White Antarctic plateau swallows glaciers
below the Circle, eats up men and horses
and civilization,

a baby in a womb. The last words of grandmothers.

Noise in a vacuum, white silent, white loud.
    It doesn't hide, bares its naked body
    for all of us, a sacrifice at the Pole.

White is trying to save us.

Clean laundry, good sweat, breath
    and green things.
Touching white loses my hand to a black hole.
Taste sand in a windstorm,
    barely noticeable but biting—bitter grit
    between teeth, that's white,
and a dead bird, still soft from the moment the car hit it.

White is a run on things, turkeys on Thanksgiving Day,
    loose change at the bus station.
White makes love to me when I'm not looking.
White is easy Easter lilies in April,
    mothers' wedding dresses, and moons.
White won't tell me the truth
    about the empty spaces it occupies.

In that way, it is my father.
White is everything outside of the lines.

White will follow me everywhere.

ROSS ISLAND

The map is blues and grays, small tips
of brown where earth is assertive.
From across the room, Ross Island
looks like a rabbit, Mt. Erebus an eye,
surprisingly, the Glacier Tongue, a tongue.
The ice shelf is barely there, a cloud
at dusk, as solid as recurring dream.
It is the shade of gray we never think about,
the place we always stand between yes and no,
solid but malleable, risky.
McMurdo Sound is blue the way oceans
are supposed to be blue— whale bones and
veins; even in my living room
the broken ice during summer
makes it darker, each shore an omen.

The map seems easily constructed,
measured, surveyed. Because I have it,
I know the men have walked
each foot of it, left their mark
and moved on. I know my feet are as guilty.

The Ross rabbit has been trampled for years now;
crossed as a challenge,
as a way to look for answers.
There are already relics there,
abandoned huts, rookeries
with ghost-penguins around them.
The rabbit wants to protect itself, run

its ruffled fur off the map, through the back patio
to the desert, if only it wasn't frozen there,
if only it wasn't established.

A CONSEQUENCE OF SOLITUDE

1

When I get to the point of counting my lover's chest hairs
laying on top of the comforter, I have reached a new low.
But it was just this morning when I crawled back into bed,
naked, and we made love with only minutes to spare before
he missed his plane, before I was late to work.
Tonight, the standard set-up for a solitary bed.
More clothes than necessary underneath the down.
When I roll over, my arm will drape where his chest would be.
All of the enemies of sleep pile on until they are
as indistinguishable as feathers,
until they cling like the want for even breathing.

Some day, I will have babies, the belly getting larger
as I breathe and run my hands over it. Babies are supposed
to be calming images. I picture the ultrasound, the big clothes,
the classes where they teach to breathe the baby out.
I picture nights when I will have a purpose, a good reason
for fluttering lids. I think about what these babies will inherit—
his eyes, my hands, and please, his sleep. Although another one like me,
someone to share nights with, that might be the thing
I am longing for. Some nights the moon is not enough.

I run circles around myself
like a dog-tail-chaser and end up in the same bare circle of carpet.
When I go to different people's houses, the insomnia turns
into curiosity. Sharing a room with a hamster and a 7-year-old
somnambulist, I realize, I am just like the 7-year-old,
but sometimes I feel like the hamster

working through the night, because that's what his body tells him
to do, carrying woodchips through tunnels, up ladders, to a house
with no roof. Could it be this easy? Could I just
switch to the night shift and find sleep during daylight hours?

2

I could take a small boat built for one, carry it across
ice floes too thick to crack with a wooden hull, make it back
to the ice where I believe I will rest. I will do anything to get there—
make bargains with people for things I don't have—
but the ice is as distant as sleep. When I return to the place
other people call home, I sleep across
the hall from a widower and his daughters. He plays
calming wave sounds all night to keep him from noticing
his wife's absence too much, to help him sleep.
I realize I am only listening to someone
else's ocean sounds, someone else's Antarctica.
What sounds will the girls choose to replace the space
their mother occupied? Perhaps I never chose,
and that keeps me here, eyes open in the dark that's dark enough
to fool me into believing they are closed. My mother dead 21 years,
theirs dead 4 months. They are already ahead of me in grieving.

After all self-pity leaves me to contemplate the islands of bed
beneath me, I am called. The mother down the hall
(not mine) in the bathroom is a grandmother, too. Even more names.
She calls because she is scared that she will need help.
She calls to get a cold cloth on her forehead, a hand on her shoulder
(don't touch me) while she retches with dry heaves, no teeth
in her mouth, dentures waiting their turn on the bathroom sink.
I have been called to watch, to wait, to help make real.
Is this what I have been trying to escape
with ice and waves and bones of the dead? I have seen
the ugly things that happen when women grow old. They lose things—

hair, teeth, body shapes, uteruses. Children. Husbands.
Control. Oh, anything but that.

If I close one eye, can I count half the amount of time as rest?
Do I age half as fast? Will I reach that breast lump
I know is coming faster if I sleep? The walk to the woods
is endless sidewalks—so how am I to return, to draw the circle
I am destined to travel? There are too many questions
keeping me up, so I plan ritual (it always worked in church):
the warm bath with long breaths and closed eyes. Music (sometimes),
warmed bed I return to out of habit, nightlight.
I tried prayer—that helped, to think of
someone listening. Then house noises begin. What I have left is ice,
and another journey. At dawn, the ice will call.

OBSERVATION HILL

Goodbye is not as easy as walking up
a steep switchback, loose gravel hinting
at my future failure, compacted snow

a more slippery message to turn back,
give it up, bless yourself and find a way
to cut your own heart out and lock it up

for all the tries you will make to get rid
of the Ice in your bones, your blood, every
in- and out-breath. With thousands of miles

between us, I can easily pretend the ice shelf
isn't still reflecting my indiscretions back
as easily as a magic mirror. I can deny

that the ice edge isn't melting a flood
into every crevasse in my body.
But here, on top of Observation Hill,

my nakedness takes me by surprise
as a phone call at 3 a.m., as a fire
that starts from an innocent candlelight

during the holidays. I am dressed in
insulation of bright memory, of shame
and raw humanity hidden in ice

crystals. When my breath catches
on the edge of my desolation,
there aren't any words to say

goodbye. There's nothing but cold
breath and resignation to be possessed
again, until the next climb.

SEARCHING FOR FAIRIES, McMURDO STATION

I searched the pressure ridges in the sea ice
thinking they'd emerge from the waters.
The monuments erected for the dead—
Vince's Cross, the cairn at Cape Evans, Scott's Cross
on Ob Hill—no fairies there.
Not at the huts either—Discovery Hut
has its mummified seals, Scott's Hut has the dog,
still chained, its skull just now
emerging from winter snowfall.

Even the populated places with footprints
and beer smells don't hold an echo of fairy, as absent as trees.
Across McMurdo Sound, Black Island is barren
and abandoned, forlorn. White island
tries its invisibility. Nothing
wants to be noticed, not even people, strangers
bundled up in red parkas, hoods covering faces.
Hiding here is the safe impossibility of anonymity.

Some people say they find God here,
behind mountains, hidden in mosaic sastrugi, even someplace
as obvious as the chapel. Fairies are harder;
they blend with snowflake, frost flower,
sparkling dust on a windy day.
Tonight a storm is building. Tomorrow morning
the roads will be dusted, new hidden slippery places.
Every time I've almost fallen, I seem to be saved.
Maybe the fairies have migrated for summer.
Tomorrow I'll check the greenhouse.

THE SOUND OF SNOW AT THE POLE

After dinner, the light comes from a part of sky
not built for diffusion, not painted for the Earth's
reflection. A walk makes this a night

for truths buried in empty station buildings
ten feet below the surface. Plates still sit
at a table as for ghosts, ceilings buckled

with the weight of so many breaths of snow,
so much deception hidden by the surface
above it. We walk out to escape the sound

of industry—the constant heavy machinery,
the power generators, the whir of airplane propellers
unable to shut down. Surprisingly, the cacophony

fills us up so that we can't even recognize ourselves
beneath the layers of clothes and naked
bravery of revelation. After dinner, we walk out,

away from station to escape. The light makes it hard
to look at anything, so we turn to sound:
the thunder of the snow under our boots

plays a summer thunderstorm memory, one
in which the sky turned green with humidity, and the air
stood still enough to smother. At Pole,

the air is restless in its secret-telling, a constant
blow to go with the snow thunder, up and away.
I wanted to be so far inside myself that night,

so far inside that parka and skin that I would not
be recognized when I emerged. I wanted the quiet
beating of my heart to be the only thing I saw.

My mistake: listening to the snow beneath your boots.

LITTLE OBLIVION

    Crabeaters in the wake,
    slow through brash to open water.
    Open like a hand can be,
    holding candy, holding
    kisses and palm lines.
    Haphazard purpose behind Ginger Island,
    between a low hill and sheer wall of glacier,
    thousands of years marbled in.
                                   The cliffs
    have a new dusting of snow and don't seem
    to care. We are searching for science,
    diet samples of Adélies, but when
    the engine stops and we drift, when penguins
    begin to porpoise with catching lunch,
    I have forgotten the memory
    of learning how to breathe
    and I let go of the rope holding me in,
    breathe as if I've just been slapped by the doctor,
    born again in this little oblivion,
    strange as any space to a child.
    The ancient newness of it all, sandstorm,
    snow.

    Easy to be lost among repeated faces,
    same faces every day, same sea,
    no, different water, same face. Same
    faces on different people, dispositions
    changeable as clothes, as the weather.
            Tobias climbs the science mast

to knock ice from the wind birds.
In the dark sky, shards fall to the deck and shatter,
little pieces of Job's mask. We all need
a science mast to wake us up, a wrench
attached to us by rope, harnesses
that will catch a jumper but will allow him to jump.
      Antarctic petrels fly by, disappear behind high waters.
Back in the place where days move
like this water, a woman is having her second
lumpectomy. Another is remembering the echo
of an ovary. A man is planning to move
his life cross-country. A granny is losing memory,
wheat fields and her husband and children, a bit
at a time. All of these get here in small packages,
easily abandoned, easily thrown overboard
to drown. The ship moves farther,
and they are all icebergs, unseemingly large
and touchless. The wind is picking up.
Soon, we will drift north.

LESSONS FROM GHOSTS

Negotiating time takes a sparrow and a drop of dog-luck;
or, in Antarctica, a skua and clear patches of sky.

To walk without falling is an easy task.
To gain Antarctica without scars is impossible;

this is why men lose their minds in the white.
When darkness chokes them with the trick of whiteness,

they see no signs of an end on the limitless plateau.
They walk forward, thinking they are walking toward rescue,

like victims under avalanche, digging themselves deeper
thinking they are headed up, to air and light.

Even the dogs know when the end is coming, want darkness
to swallow them as quickly as it has tricked the men to die.

The dog-ghosts arrive on wingtip with full-color sight
and joy in understanding the intimacies of white.

The man-ghosts refuse to let go, mules of habit,
wandering between white and darkness, wind-blown bluff to ice shelf.

We think we have learned when we stumble through the wind
in winter that breaks windows and buries what we think of

as survival: computers, phones, extreme cold weather gear
freezing in offices adrift with the remnants of a blizzard.

In all our safety, we remain snowblind, tricked
into believing Antarctica is ours. We remain,

gripping the ice as if we were saving it, when we
are the ones being held, possessed;

we all remain, like snow dust in the wind,
clinging to ice like any good bird stays with an updraft.

SAYING GOODBYE TO THE CONTINENT

Even though you've found your way
north, moving up through the Gerlache,
and even though your hand on the ship
and your eyes on the glacier are saying goodbye,
you are not leaving this continent.
She will not leave you.
Just like the lost teddy bear at seven, or that first sex,
Antarctica will stay.

Saying goodbye won't do.
You know you'll be back, even if your body
never crosses 60 south again.

The voice of glacier, hands of water
beg you not to leave. Believe them
when they say you are the best thing
that ever happened to them, but then,
they are saying this as you are leaving.

As you steam north through the South Pacific,
feel her, a lump in your body,
how she clings everywhere on this ship.
She whispers to you in those moments before sleep,
when legs twitch with memory,
here, I'm still here, you will find me again.

Best not to question comings and leavings.
Best to go like all the others,
ice in their blood, ice always in their minds.

CRACK IT OPEN

Wildflower orchid, this continent,
as terrained, delicate and open-mouthed,
a misplaced home. It opened like a flower,
a woman for the men looking to conquer
her. The ice catches all our fallen grace
in its cracks, all the explorers asking
for another chance to love her. Women
know the fragility of ice, as glass
or a breast lump, ready to crack open.
We hear it calling, think about sisters
and hidden naked bodies on a snow-
covered beach. We are with it, in all its
fallen glory, the ice. Our bodies
cracked and weeping for open water.

ACKNOWLEDGMENTS

Grateful acknowledgment is made to the following journals in which some of these poems originally appeared:

Elixir: "Turtle Rock, Antarctica," "When Ice Catches Daylight, Addiction," and "What the Ice Knows"
Isotope: "Survival School," "Going Through the Gerlache," and "The Beacon Valley"
RUNES: A Review of Poetry: "Lessons From Ghosts"
Marlboro Review: "Heading to Dion Island, Antarctica" and "The Body of Ice Remembered"
Image: A Journal of Arts and Religion: "Seven Attempts at Observation Hill"
Clackamas Literary Review: "Going to the Seal Rodeo" and "What Happens During Whiteouts in Antarctica"
Borderlands: Texas Poetry Review: "Little Oblivion" and "Saying Goodbye to the Continent"
Boulevard: "Naming the Bird"
Black Warrior Review: "Going to Pole"
Louisiana Literature: "Ross Island"
New England Review: "Riverbed Warnings of Birth by Accident" and "Swallowing Antarctica"
Santa Clara Review: "Southern Ocean, Fairies, and Winter Solstice"

"Swallowing Antarctica," and "Weightlessness in a Red Parka" appeared in the anthology *Deep Travel: Contemporary American Poets Abroad* (Ninebark Press, 2007).

Susan Allspaw is a writer and editor who also works as an information security professional. She has read poetry on Senator Bill Bradley's radio show "American Voices" and has been to Antarctica four times. She serves as copy editor for *The Antarctic Sun*, and continues to support the US Antarctic Program.

TITLES FROM ELIXIR PRESS

POETRY

Circassian Girl by Michelle Mitchell-Foust
Imago Mundi by Michelle Mitchell-Foust
Distance From Birth by Tracy Philpot
Original White Animals by Tracy Philpot
Flow Blue by Sarah Kennedy
A Witch's Dictionary by Sarah Kennedy
The Gold Thread by Sarah Kennedy
Monster Zero by Jay Snodgrass
Drag by Duriel E. Harris
Running the Voodoo Down by Jim McGarrah
Assignation at Vanishing Point by Jane Satterfield
Her Familiars by Jane Satterfield
The Jewish Fake Book by Sima Rabinowitz
Recital by Samn Stockwell
Murder Ballads by Jake Adam York
Floating Girl (Angel of War) by Robert Randolph
Puritan Spectacle by Robert Strong
Keeping the Tigers Behind Us by Glenn J. Freeman
Bonneville by Jenny Mueller
Cities of Flesh and the Dead by Diann Blakely
The Halo Rule by Teresa Leo
Perpetual Care by Katie Cappello
The Raindrop's Gospel: The Trials of St. Jerome and St. Paula by Maurya Simon
Prelude to Air from Water by Sandy Florian
Let Me Open You A Swan by Deborah Bogen
Cargo by Kristin Kelly
Spit by Esther Lee
Rag & Bone by Kathrym Nuernberger

Kingdom of Throat-stuck Luck by George Kalamaras
Mormon Boy by Seth Brady Tucker
Nostalgia for the Criminal Past by Kathleen Winter
Little Oblivion by Susan Allspaw
Quelled Communiqués by Chloe Joan Lopez
Stupor by David Ray Vance

FICTION

How Things Break by Kerala Goodkin
Nine Ten Again by Phil Condon
Memory Sickness by Phong Nguyen
Troglodyte by Tracy DeBrincat

LIMITED EDITION CHAPBOOKS

Juju by Judy Moffat
Grass by Sean Aden Lovelace
X-testaments by Karen Zealand
Rapture by Sarah Kennedy
Green Ink Wings by Sherre Myers
Orange Reminds You Of Listening by Kristin Abraham
In What I Have Done & What I Have Failed To Do by Joseph P. Wood
Hymn of Ash by George Looney
Bray by Paul Gibbons